TRIALS OF POETRY

MADALINA DAY

NEW BEGINNINGS THERAPY

DEDICATION: TO MY CHILD

CONTENTS

FOREWORD

Random

Poetry: Past, Present And Future

INTRODUCTION

Trials of poetry are lyrical episodes presented as an opening dialogue or correspondence on the subject of *love*. Keywords and white blank pages are symbolic of reflective spaces, inviting to examine and continue an imaginary compositional journey. Conceptual basis of this work is rooted in an assessment of the **value of poetry** and its potential **accessibility** as a literary genre.

Trials of poetry speaks of freedom, limitless imagination, and a need for reciprocity in the creative process, making a parallel with **love** as a relationship between two people. It also poses a question on whether a strong desire to express love through lyrics as a medium is enough and or sufficient in crafting an accomplished script. And what if that communication never makes it to its destination? Would that then diminish the message and or its value? **Ways of communicating rather than communication itself takes center stage.**

PROLOGUE

*"to love when loved is when
writing on a flowing stream"*

APPEARING ASLEEP 2007–2008

Long time it seems
The past few minutes; of a life inside, lost in my own
small world.
Life is not always what it seems,
There is one book I can now recall.

Late but early morning, a cent down for thoughts
Two strings of plastic
Closing down a lamppost
Wish that was you still, but it was only a Robot.

At four in the morning,
Flight thoughts are awakening
There are no snowmen about
As spring and the sound of it has come…

Quiet, all white and silence; relaxing sejour awaiting
repeat.

FAITHLESS
2007–2008

If you are my artist,
One thing I did today:
Remembering and reckoning how to pray

THE GARDENER
2007–2008

Tremendous sounds from the bells within,
At half-past eleven, a pray awaits,
Under the candles finds no faith
There was no one's hand to (neither) hold nor say

Singing, the snow was covering the gardener
Stepped outside,
Each second, knowingly, not serving the mystery of
inside

My friend was to be "availed" beyond my doubts;
A milk coffee and poverty of words to say the last
Good Night
A severe Good Bye without excess.

DISLIKING POLITENESS 2009

Why it's just so hard to say: no?
Doubtless much easier if followed by thanks
And if one adds "sorry", somehow,
Completed it's the charade for: no, thank you.

DOING WORDS: 2009

Reading what was written months and months ago,
By me and by you,
Us,
Again and again
Making love with words and of words
Thoughts surfing skin, wetness in a mouth

Penetrating images are wandering,
Touches are closing in,
So near, so tight.
Connecting, wishes are text
And soon, dark becomes a satisfying light.
After a while, ready, you say:
Thank you, Good Night.

Now,
On their knees, desires turn to sadness
Pleasure's leftovers are dry paint memories,
Or at least that is all that can be conceived of it now.

Are the lights going to scream their way through?

When is the pain going to go away?
Where?
I remembered.

DISENGAGED
2010

Fear, look: Tears have gone away,
End of the road.
Quiet noise,
Background to a life; colourless hope.

It shouldn't be any other way.
Sometime soon,
Diffuse sound will embrace a startling ray of light.

Shadows are moving ahead of time
Calming wall as new order of things
There is your picture in every smile.

HAPPINESS WITHOUT A QUESTION MARK? 2010

Spreading its wings across
Let a smile be born from within
Convincingly speaking out:
Happiness without a question mark

A VIEW ACROSS THE READING LINES 2010

Not long ago
Simple words, kind gestures, gentle touches
Mind browsing, libraries searches, suave poems,
Great writers, classic novels and

Wind swings, mood swings,
I still do: I love you.
So much more every day…

UNRESOLVED
2010

A passing stranger,
Feelings and desolate emotions
For a moment I thought was you.
While standing, have asked:
Please, don't look back,
There was but nothing there, then.
While longing for a kiss, memories return untouched…

UNJUSTIFIED
2010

Tears at the end of an eye
One travels down
And deep marks are left behind.
Hand goes up soothing a whisper of hope
Blushing, in a corner, solitude stands
Brave, encouraging itself seeks company at once

There is still a long way!
Thought goes…
There isn't any time for repose,
Entangled, nearby, innocence skipping
Naively, offers a friendship.

Light and bright senses are cheering
Illuminating all is well and expected to continue.
Something interferes
Forward moves.

LANDSCAPE OF A SOUL 2010

Where are you? I'm lost, can't find <u>core</u>.
Where is the beginning of me?
Did thought start when you?
No?
Then I was wrong,

Once and again.

PREFERENCE ON ONCE UPON A TIME 2009

Once upon a time
There was a book of fairy tales
Page after page, characters were coming alive.
There was this timid and *clear* Voice declaring loves.
Receiving end, bluntly and frankly said:
I can hear you, but cannot see you and I don't reciprocate.
Without resentment and not ashamed Voice parted.

Around that time Voice being terribly hurt asked for help.
Sadly, help was not to be given as Voice was believed rather unwell.

Beginning of a story about unrequited love
Sadness set aside, regrets left behind
Questioning starts another story whereas
Truth is not compelled to be revealed

All is covered up.

Why? Voice should wonder, if ever encounters chance.
Misunderstandings, confusion, loss of faith are (re) interpreted and replaced.
Deep, hidden, subconscious awakes only to find deserted, lifeless dunes of sand.

Is that the end? No, that cannot be!

Voice speaks…

MOVING ON 2010

I never thought I could say this while remembering the emptiness of your heart:

Dark, subdued, tacit (mis)understandings

Today, there is much the water sees…

FORGIVENESS
2010

Take my hand, don't ask.

Won't let you down, not now not ever,

I that I am is more than you think.

Take it, won't ask again, it will be there for when you need it.

CONSTANT CLARIFICATION 2010

Trail of ideas, in print onto an endless path

Pictures and signs within an unlimited discourse of fantasy

Imagination runs wild.

A whirl, in flux movements,

Perspectives are intertwined and hard to read.

Something is missing, decipher is blurred

Symbol of captivity attached to a poll.

Unlike air, freedom is confined.

Is it too late if understanding is on standby?

Invisible, strong spirited presence,

Standing – Discovering

Link to our future and answer to our past.

The little things that make one happy: Dreams.

Open your mind and hold your heart high.

MISSING YOU IN CONVERSATION: 2010

I thought of you today…

You looked surprised, many unspoken words in your eyes.

My fingers were gently drawing new lines on your lips

Desires prevail: Please, hold me in!

Exhausting recall on what you once said

As a consequence, at present, there are countless books beside my bed.

Can that knowledge be found?

Could that experience be lived?

I'm going back to bed

Shall I feel deceived?

No, I dare, I dare dreams to be relived.

LEARNING A LANGUAGE THROUGHOUT 2011

What way shall we take next?

Latin and, going all the way back.

Today's sense is building on syllables of past times:

Qvo Vadis.

WILDERNESS WHILE CROSSING 2010

Disappointment is not something that should be consciously searched, however, every now and then stone after stone and step after step inevitably various challenges are found. Moving on and only regrets left behind—don't look back.

For when you are enabled,

Constraints vanish and simplicity takes place

BLISS 2011

Every day I feel so very lucky only by just looking at you.

The times you are smiling make me strong

My suppositions of what it is to be a mother are reinforced.

Somehow, together, we clarify the beauty of life

Its challenges, important reminiscences of our lives

You, my child, bring dreams alive!

TO THE ONE I MISS: 2010

Let me be, she says turning on her side
Why persevere?
Determination to see this through it will only twist
things
It won't bring truth.

When I stopped pain, I stopped all...

Searching for new meanings,
Flesh not decomposed,
Tangible and conceivable
Without feeling loss
Affection reinstated brings unghost.

Solemn speeches are conceived born out of forgive-
ness:

Sublime refuge

JOURNEY 2011

That stare, that look,

It made me feel so perfectly happy

Privileged uncertainty

Emotion not motion

Train journey into one's life;

FALLING 2010

Until the end there was another time: next time.
Until the end thought sought another chance
Until the end there was choice to be made
Until the end I simply wished to see you once, again.

NOT ABOUT 2010

It is not about what we meant for one another,

It is not about promises, delusions but rather

Myriad of happenings while still holding on

PRACTICALITIES
AND DECEPTION
2010

Cutting slow
Incisions into a heart
Left chamber feeling a pulse
Words tattooed underneath a strapless bra.

'So long, my dear,' he said
'Nothing means something to me, but you…'

She was not listening
Her vision replaced by ravaging pain
Instead of heartbroken she discovered that
It was easier if you don't let anyone define who you
are!

Years later, they met again.
She was blessed and with another.
He was content to see her but it did not matter.
At the end everyone seemed happy.

CHRISTMAS LIGHTS 2010

All over town
Far too early and not soon enough
Much to wish for, another year around

NOT TOO
LATE 2010

You thought you took our world with you

Just like that
But then again,
The only thing you took away (eliminate) is yourself
(YOU)
Can you see it now?

Can you see at all?

No? That is what I thought!
Pity it's not my stand. So stay with that, stay statue.

OVER AND OVER 2011

Strands of repetitions aligned in geometrical order
Creating patterns, differing sides, prioritising and re-
thinking
Never ending duties.
Responsibilities and homonyms sounds
Quilt of life with no possibility of quitting.

Open your eyes and now, close your eyes.
What can you see?
What can you imagine?

PARALLEL TO ME 2011

Do you remember our walk through the park?
It took us some years,
It has been sinister and rather quiet
Endorsed by numerous symbols, random names
Solitarily on trees skin
Encrypted **bark**

Spontaneous emotions transferred, pro—into the air
We picked each other's signals
I, misguided, was reading into my heart.
You were preoccupied, not much,
After all, for you, it was just a walk into the park.

REBUS 2011

Collapsed, in reverie, for some time now
Can't decide between pictures in my mind
Rich autumn,
Splendid weather,
My son is picking up seasonal leaves
On the other side
Night's tragedy unfolds
So much to see, so much to uphold
Looking back,
A silhouette unveiled, nude and in much pain.

There are no answers but memories of past times.

KEYWORDS:

Ashore
Tide approaching
Preconscious
Cliffs
Witness
Faded
Unsure

BEFORE
SOLITUDE

Another tide, another moment has passed
Why is time measured in sand?
The sea is quiet now
Grey and darkness absorbed
Ashore, remains
As the only witness to my heart.

Zbuciumul se inchide, calm insine
Stancile nesigure raman imbatranite.

Translation:
The turmoil quietly and silently closes: calm self
Uncertain rocks continue

ANEW 2011

Dignity,

Long searched for

Enslaved by both social concepts and economic contracts

Bandaging, covering invisible wounds

A whole body of work

Like a long corridor of hanging mirrors

And if walked through: images,

Foreseen happenings with glimpses of a you and

Fatigued, dusted frames of time embracing each and every distortion

Everything is inscribed

For that that cannot be read it has not been written yet.

PARAMOUNT
2011

Diamond shapes

Agitated clusters of knowledge, reshaping, renaming

Immersed
Leaning over

There was a way out
For truth to come through
Distinguishing what was palpable and real
Like a child, she covered her eyes,
Like a child, she covered her ears.

Light

BRIDGE 2011

Long time ago, too long to be said but not too long to be remembered

In a country, far away and with no name

There was a

THOUGHT
PERFECTION 2011

Senses aligned, a perfect vertical
Their hands holding on to each other's bodies
Loosen,
Warm protective scarves for times to come
It did not look like an embrace, at first anyway,
But it was; it was something thought out and lived of
the kindest way.

Standing across, your desk still in the middle

All I could think

Genuine, unaware,

UNDER AUSTERITY TIMES: WHERE ONE EARNS THE RIGHT TO BREATHE: THE UNITED KINGDOM

Clouds gathered together
The sound of thunder drums resonating to far ends
A land believed hopeless it proved, instead, on being crude
The followed *steps*
Surrounding buildings stagnated on reveries of time
Like politics slipping on oil grounds

At first, thought was obscure and filled with sorrow
Only projections of vast Nordic winds
Dissecting, reaching to Celestial altitudes;

Austerious, trial after trial, scenario inquisitively un-
wrapped
Everything that was meant to be seen

and behold.

Poverty hidden on rich people's sleeves.
Ill manners dressed on velvety expressions aimed at
naïve ears and/or lonely accents of a tongue
Decadence found a new dimension depending on
one's heart.
Do you want more?
Because, more is what there is: not all is emotionless,
indoctrinated and unaware of what.

Nevertheless everyone says: all is well!
There is a new Century ahead of us.
Question is: do we still have time?

Memory line priestly answers: :history as we have
known it allows for carrying on".

However, pessimist or intellectual souls disagree.
In between, culturally and economically trapped,
She stood as void
There was no hope without a mind of heart.

Then, there and for eternity the search for belonging
had come to its end:

There was no hope when there was no heart! and
there is no heart in this Kingdom.

PROGRESSION 2011

When early

I wonder about you sometimes, in fact: I wonder about you quite a lot!

How you are, what have you been doing; all that is (possibly) new with you.

I do wonder about you sometimes and will I ever see you again.

I'm wondering that.

KEY TO A NEW VERSE, RECALL:

EMBRACE ALL THAT'S WITHIN:

Positive
Harmony
Shield
Aura
Blessings
In awe
In love
Desire
Wishful
Thoughtful
Brightness
Senses
Clarity
Hopeful
Sensations
Sentimental
Natural
Chance
Energy
Stimulus

Various
Standpoints
Core
Intensity
Care

BEING ENOUGH

Acceptance,

Developing understanding

Friendship on return

Chair – significance

Nonchalant

YOUR BIRTHDAY

So I remembered, I did not want to but it happened anyway.

I know it is your birthday and I also know that I won't do anything about it.

Shall I contact you now that I remembered?

Never crossed my mind

So it's your birthday and I did not want to know but I remembered anyway.

HEALING

She was battered and on the ground
With no tears coming out,
She looked up before she looked down and looked all
around

He was smiling, he did it again and satisfaction out
She would not leave, not again, not with her child
still asleep.

Nevertheless, in time, good time, she re-learned her
ways, she got stronger and she was more than able to
stand
But all that was love, love to her, died
Certainly, unquestionably and slowly deep deep in-
side.

THE NIGHT'S SIGHS

Wonder: Tell me about the sea, the sea's blue eyes, still blue eyes?

BEING 16 - STYLE AND FEAR - FIRST LOVE

What else can I tell you? What else is there to say? What else can I tell the one that holds all my whispers? What does the seagull tells the sea wave for which it loves its eternity?

Nothing....it just rotates in the blue hourglasses with its dance touching its waves. Who's dancing? The Seagull? The Wave?

Do you know where do you begin and where do you end? My dream....I wish to see it in flight. Are you going to help?

RESPONSIBLE IMAGINATION

Happy reflections

Key words

Bulb Soil Green
Cherished
Open up
Pictorial
Murmur
Warm Dreams

WHY?

Open up the window to my soul
And you will see
A scarlet rose dressing it up
And as the day is passing by
A sense of loss is withered away

MAZE

For so long alienated
It has taken many turns of moons

Until we found each and for now, an other;
Reminiscences of your first glance on me;
It felt unpredictable and delightful
To us both, hope says…
Were we already to be meant?
No, of course, that cannot be a written thought!

I'm certain that while looking at you looking at me it
felt like petals of flowers coming through
Climbing and then
Blossom.
Foolish, sweet romance of a heart
Flower to your lips, flower to your eyelids,
Flower to your ears, flower to your forehead
Flower to your chicks
Flower to your senses
All receiving seemingly surreal codes
Absorbing, emanating and divulging
Magic done and undone
With words and into the skin

Where are you now?
Soft silk…

DOUBLE NEGATIVE AND BEING NAÏVE

Nothing was real and yet, it was not a dream either
My thoughts are searching for you, for so long now,
I can hear my heart wishing aloud with such intensity but,
Only memories are there as to answer,
Echoing and completing the unsaid
Nothing was real and yet, I know it was not a dream either.

GOING BACK AND FROM BEFORE

Why things were so much easier before?
Probably because I felt that you were listening,
Even if for a short while
Why were we so much happier?
Probably because

2009 REMEMBER!

I have a confession to make:

Last night I stripped

First I took off my wedding band and with it nine long years of a ring

Then I released my neck of a chain holding on to lost beliefs,

Within seconds I was nude and confused

Only childbirth scars that could not be removed

2009 REMEMBER THE REST:

Jump—Life starts with numbers

Jump! Jump if you can

Swim in the blue waters of ocean and life

WRITINGS, PENSIVE AND OTHERWISE

Dragostea noastra,
Our love,
like a snowflake adrift in vast unknown
By a sea current desire
Running towards each other
We met halfway.
How long is it going to take from now... Dreams

MAX: HOUSE OF FLOWERS

DREAM

LONGING

MISSING MATHS

World of exact things with acknowledged chance for errors

SNOWDROPS

Keywords/ picture

Bulb Soil Green Cherished
Open up Pictorial Murmur Warm Dreams

Snowdrops on patches of grass
Shy and rising above freezing grounds
Sign of homecoming Spring
Queen of all
 with snow melting under warm glances of a sun.

Children joyfully dragging their school bags
With music on their lips, and ready for assemblies
Books to be read, spellings to be learned
Maths memorised
Science accomplishing awareness to most unpredict-
able sides.

ANOTHER SEASON

LOVE
PRESCRIPTION

Ms. Jane Hope
Please ensure intake of 500 milligrams of
Three times a day
Preferably, after main meals
Breakfast—for up to 9am
Lunch—any time between 12pm and 1pm
Dinner—random and for about 7pm

Possible side effects and most encountered: **Smiles**!
Defined as completely out of order and probably irri-
tating others around!
—meaning the ones most nearby…
If not encouraged, such side effects should wear off
within a sensible amount of time.

SEEING THROUGH

Keywords:

Interpretation
Motivation
Veil
Clarity
Reflection
Choice
Positive Desire
Wishful
Tolerance
Learning
On other sides
Essential

Tasting life
Every moment

NOT AS IT WAS
THOUGHT
NOR MEANT

WISHES OF
ALL 2007

Her name was Hope and she was born of change
Allusive, endearing and with signs of hope
That journey had begun

She did not know it all, she was uncertain until it was too late. Hope wondered how she could change things and make it all better. Transcribing what had happened and understanding her journey. Last memory she had of them together was grey, black and white shaded lines on a book page—unidentifiable language.

Encrypted on her mind, much was to come alive and substance, identifiable realities but of a different time; something was terribly wrong, she could not explain it but it was profoundly, deeply felt. Close by, present but not tangible—a sense of loss. It was regrettable, that disassociation and her memories…

She missed you so very much, so much so that she decided never to revisit that memory, that time some time ago.

Such loss, most incomprehensible to human heart...

Questions asked and questions answered, that evening on an underground platform.

Stern expressions, repressed emotions of all kinds with trains yet to arrive and depart—"there is not going to be another chance"—it was such an echo in her mind:" this is goodbye."

KEYWORDS:

Interpretations
Symbols Memory How?
Why?
Forward
Consciousness
Integrity
Her forgiveness as key to all that need remembered

Alleviation

Keywords

Sunrise Surprising Amusing Sensible Witty Relaxed
Distinctive

13:10

Recover what was once love, what was once lost
Time brings around moments,
One and then another
Decide.

Recover what was once precious, deeply

Profunzimea gandurilor tale
Le-am intalnit
In colturi intunecate, virgine In mine.
Atunci si acum, recent.
Lasand un trail of ideas

ICICLES AND BEAUTY

Nature,
Never cease to amaze nor beatify
Cave icicles forming clear, memorable frozen moments of time
From above, water drops, dignified Stalactites
So much
Strong, natural sculptures rising

Stalagmites

CHILDREN OF THE VILLAGE 2011

Keywords

Green hills, lake, calming water welcoming recent rain
Troubadour/travellers—horse cart selling wooden goods/spoons
Tobacco fields, village paths, grandparents' house, Porch

MEMORY'S WRINKLES

Childhood imagines reconstructed
Past images recycled onto today's fabric of a dream
And, if not careful,
Persecuting rather than delighting.

Remembered are the green hills,
Remembered is the lake on the edgy valley with its
calming water welcoming each and every new tear
rain from above

While troubadours and travellers were discovering,
exploring country grounds
In their horse cart, selling artisan wooden goods
Defeating present, despotic political rules and its
rulers
Children of the village were running, wild, announcing the newcomers
Tobacco fields forming both background and sharp
contrast to an ancient way of life.

Remembered are grandparents' houses on black and

white pictures
Immortal scenes
Capturing church bells -
Pity though, as images are unable to transpose the sacred missives sent out all around
Bell sounds.

Remembered are unusual portraits on each porch, new water wells just found,
The fire lit evenings with summer supper served out on verandas
Irreplaceable, home baked foods and mystical aromas

When to terms, evening dance would start
Youngsters will raise and build their future paths.

KEYWORDS:

Stronger
Sense Open
Indulgent
Motivation Search end
Beginning
Afresh

Keywords

Vulnerable Tolerant
Susceptible
Caress
Dim recall
Enhance

PETUNIA 2012

Third sunset of the year was proudly/profoundly claiming its time
Sun went into hiding
Grounds were once again left uncrowned
And in this part of the world
Night was persuading day and day was persuading night...

Hills covered on fiery bronze light
Enhancing, assisting, landscapes were formed.

Encapsulating moments, movements
Trees as witnesses
Leaning their necks, bowing respectfully
My hands, long arms reaching

Air, deluding, truthfully much holding on
Oh, no!
Where are you?
Why existing, even if, briefly only in my dreams?
I was over you, and in so many ways you were long gone
But, not so much so, right now...

I sense you again

Soft wind undulating tree leaves
Somehow pleasuring all around
Don't let green tear drops rain on us unless that promised
given note finally left on our bench it is no longer wandering adrift, aloof like

KEYWORDS

Sensible
Happy
Decisive
Balance Hopeful
Patience
Emotions
Forward
Life
Water

Immaculate
Purity
Repositioning/Reintegration
Ahead of time
Mountains
Creation
Futility
Fertile mind
Form
Sense

LOVERS' POEM

"I love you" was never said

KEYWORDS:

Red card
Steps

MERMAIDS' FOUNTAIN

Keywords:

Fountain in the square
Art gallery
Windows
Cafés,
Coffee shops
Awake, vibrant atmosphere
Bridge
Market
Olive trees
Sounds
Celebration

IF I WERE A POEM…

Every poem has a story to tell,
Would you believe me if I say: This one doesn't?

Every poem has a story to tell,
Do you believe me if I say: This one doesn't?!

KEYWORDS

Library
Hardcover book
Pages
Consummated hunger
Message
Source of life

Dressed and veiled, breath after breath
Inescapable

POEM OF TIMES TO COME 2011

She turned around
Her smile fresh with lips murmuring a deeply felt
love
Her mind was no longer fighting through dark mem-
ories
Breathing... the sound of her calm calling
This time was a time to come around and stay
Stay with her for an infinity
An infinity of moments—

She knew...
There was an eye with sight
A clear thought followed by an image
A memory of past time into a near future

Chance aloud becoming reality
Posture addressed her voice tempered and ready
She was I ...
Her verse was encrypted... a language long lost in
mystery
Intensity exacerbated by rapid movement

Protector to a side and friend on the other

There was a time and time again
That moment captured in her heart
Split second and fragments of unimaginable being
Began a journey in sound
Imperceptible
Music condensed, her being absorbing and answer-
ing

Her new beginnings, her name was loud and alive
Her choice, her being
A present for a past
She knew then that she were never to be alone…
Her life… an eye to I
Deeply rooted for an eternity of time.

Eyes open allowing for a new love to come
Unexpected we met the next day
For the first time
Love at sight, felt and declared
A gentle touch of hearts.
Passion developed in what it seemed days
The very fact but only seconds in real time.

KEYWORDS

Light
Interpretation
Dynamic
Reverie
Present
Calm
Encouraging
Love
Clarity
Surroundings
Childhood
Mother
Identity
Responsibilities
Revisiting
Always
Mind
Emotions
Verse
Creative

KEYWORDS 1.1

Happiness
Accomplished
Journey
Life
Nourishment
Bonheur
Colour
Visit
Presents
Hearts

KEYWORDS 1.12

Past
Resolved
Music
Soothing
Sense and I
Growth
Development
Empirical
Real

TOUCHING, IMAGES OF YOU AND I

Closing. Gentleness much tenderness
Full stop and a new beginning
She rushed through
clippings scissors and shapes of paper
Random dressing forming, composing
She becomes a tree
Drawing into becoming a thought
A thought developing a her, dressed in dreams
Her dreams visible and real
An inversion and conversion, past to real and real to
past into becoming
There is an embrace.
Kissed into being born

 …dancers gathering she founds her density
Composing
Melody from abyss catapulting itself
Contour shapes her fragility into defining

Eyes met… it's not too early… it's really not too late
….

BRIDGES INTO SHAPES

Seven towers seven angles for a thought

Uncontrollable creative brush painting away

Power of blue and power of red

Practice into being... a circle complete
All wonders in that world into her palm
brushing painting and depicting

Stories forming and reshaping
The power of red and her power of blue
Calming embracing her passion, her love

An old oak outside her window offering shade
Serenading her into sleep

KEYWORDS

I power and love

Acceptance and redirecting darkness to its origin of
faith
Hands moving undulating
Sparring unfearful love

Image
Picture
Glimpse
Grey wonder
Life
Readjustment
Power of life- reabsorbing into I
Bending with power of water blue and red re-joined

Morning dew, unstoppable rain cleansing
Remains of uncertainty in her soul
Path opening allowing light and wisdom
He was standing outside right corner of her sight
Visible, strong impetuous presence
A gentle reminder, unique connections in her mind

MAI was her name—her first syllable of her time

Name with a vision, name with a sound—she alone stands for beginning
She alone stands for a new life
Many around her, without wisdom tried to hurt and pain her
Even when her willingness said I let you go, this once
Trespassing is not allowed but I can see your weakness…
Her wisdom was not for sale, her wisdom was not a bargain
Her wisdom was for those that she loved.
Everyone else tricked themselves into believing that she failed

Next day, another day, a new beginning sought to life
Light, blessings and a child's laughter—her child…

REMINISCING
2010

My heart, my love, my dreams clustered into my wishes
Like paced pedestrians awaiting a green light
Signalling its sound, perceptible confusion.
I picked up my child and walked like a Tess
Not sparing a look,
A chance and without a doubt.
My life encumbered in imposed beliefs—I take them off
Unlike before when Barefooted, for all next days, I walk my way into happiness

Seconds later, envisaging a life in light, my questions have choices beyond unquestionable answers
Fringe of time is felt upon whilst running up a hill, a something clambered and climbed
The joys of discovery,

A sense of self revived, relived sublime refuge of my mind
Unleashed my light holds tight

There is so much hope
So much all within and around.

GLIMMER OF
HOPE

Sometime soon we arrive to be as we were then
A **_Then_** that we do not know when what we want it is
to become
Scattered **_Words_** over a vast indefinite **_X_**
A name untouched of foreign understandings
And Alone and Quiet
A gentle, soft inclination
An unpredictable blessed wonder
For things to come.

My heart, my love, my dreams all in one
Clear water, compassionate murmur of my whispers
I embrace you again
Into a future of hope
Confidently walking a path
Becoming what I belong:
Core of strength.

Cindva am ajuns sa fim ca noi atunci/ sometime soon
we arrive to be as we were then
Un atunci care nu stim cand ceea ce vrem va deveni/

a then that we not know when what we want it is to become

Cuvinte imprastiate pe un neant nedefinit/ scattered words over a vast indefinite x

Un nume nepatruns de intelesuri straine/ a name untouched of foreign understandings

Si singure, in tacere/ and alone and quiet

O aplecare lina, a gentle, soft inclination

O strangere neprevazuta,

an unpredictable blessed wonder

For things to come

My heart, my love, my dreams all in one   Accomplished and indeplinite.

Apa cristalina/clear water

Sopotul ingaduitor al gandurilor mele,/compassionate murmur of my thoughts

Te imbratisez din nou si din nou, I embrace you again and again

Into a future of hope

Mergand in confidenta pe o cale/confidently walking a path

O viata implinita, fara dezamagiri si fara regrete

Devenind ceea ce sunt

Core of strength

Singuratatea nu are raspuns Dar eu, acum

Are.

My heart, my love, my dreams. in devenire

SENSE 2008

A turning, felt less abrupt with hands wavering a truth
Normality, a life adjusted to its comings
My strength…
There was a vision close path to memories
Innocuous and entangled approach
Cleared
Blue skies, an opening of a story
Decades later.
Widened

Allowing for a chorus
a song composed

2016 END OF AN ERA

Source of life—end of an era

I am looking at the world with an open heart
There is an image of a child that I carried on my back
He was five and I felt young
I wondered how long for and it was known
For the rest of life, my life
but not on my back, and as always facing me, looking
and gazing and I would assure my response back—
to start with on parts, feeding and feeding from the
best of hearts.
I am looking at the world with an open heart
Like that very first second of life someone was reach-
ing up
Closing and wanting and existing not only within
and not only without
Realising that
What was then continues now and the rest of days
I am looking at the world with an open heart and I
have to teach
To teach my child, first to breathe and feed and exist

within me and soon enough to remind him that his world has meanings and he has meanings and many more meanings can be found

I am looking at the world with an open heart and then I know that being open at heart is not enough

Possibly enough only in my heart;

I need to let him know that now I know

I know that now, I knew it then and I know it again

He needs to learn how to open his heart, to open his heart to a world that is not always going to feed him back

He needs to open his heart to a world that he may, at times, find unkind even to the best of hearts

I have to teach my child to open his heart to a world that sometimes has meanings and that sometimes more or different meanings can be found within self and outside

That is my very lesson, my very lesson to my only child about a world, our world and how to open his heart.

This is me at this very stage…

WHEN THERE
IS TIME 2007

When there is time
When your mind is healed
When your heart is filled with happiness and joy
When you hold hope at the tip of your fingers
Today I am awake with calmness of all kinds
Smiling is on my mind
When there is time.

Printed in Great Britain
by Amazon